THE

ORIENTAL RACES AND TRIBES,

Residents and Visitors of Bombay,

A SERIES OF PHOTOGRAPHS,

WITH LETTER-PRESS DESCRIPTIONS

THE

ORIENTAL RACES AND TRIBES,

Residents and Visitors of Bombay,

A SERIES OF PHOTOGRAPHS,

WITH LETTER-PRESS DESCRIPTIONS.

BY WILLIAM JOHNSON

IN TWO VOLUMES
VOL. I. - GUJARAT, KUTCH, AND KATHIAWAR.

GYAN

Published by

Gyan Publishing House
5, Ansari Road
Daryaganj, New Delhi-110002
Phone: 011-47034999, 9811692060
E-mail: books@gyanbooks.com

Distribution Network
gyanbooks.com
India, USA, Canada, UK, Australia

ISBN: 978-81-212-5570-7 (Set)
978-81-212-5571-4 (HB)
First Published, 1863

2nd Impression 2024

Printed at: Gyan Press, Delhi.

THE ORIENTAL RACES AND TRIBES, RESIDENTS AND VISITORS OF BOMBAY, A SERIES OF PHOTOGRAPHS, WITH LETTER-PRESS DESCRIPTIONS (VOL. I)

Author: WILLIAM JOHNSON

THE ORIENTAL RACES AND TRIBES.

VOL. I.

GUJARÂT KUTCH, AND KÂTHIAWÂR.

THE

ORIENTAL RACES AND TRIBES,

Residents and Visitors of Bombay.

A SERIES OF PHOTOGRAPHS,

WITH LETTER-PRESS DESCRIPTIONS.

BY WILLIAM JOHNSON.

BOMBAY CIVIL SERVICE (UNCOV.)

VOL. I.—GUJARÂT, KUTCH, AND KÂTHIAWÂR.

LONDON:

W. J. JOHNSON, 83 AND 121, FLEET STREET; AND BOLTON AND BARNITT, 146, HOLBORN BARS.

1863.

ILLUSTRATIONS.

PREFACE.

OF Bombay, more than of London in the eye of the poet Cowper, it may be truthfully said—

> "Oh, thou resort and mart of all the earth,
> Chequered with all complexions of mankind."

In that great and wealthy city, supposed to be now the most populous in India, faces are to be seen of every variety of hue, from that of the fair northern European to that of the tropical African, nearly as black as ebony. It contains numerous representatives of almost all the races and tribes of the Indian Continent and Islands. It has, every season, numerous visitors from the countries of Central Asia, and from even remoter lands. "It is not only from its commercial prosperity," says Sir John Malcolm, "that such persons resort to it, but from its being the port to which all the inhabitants of Arabia, Persia, Mekran, and part of Affghanistan, first come; as also that by which all pass that either go from India to those countries, or who proceed on a pilgrimage to Mecca, Kerbela, or Nijif. In the whole course of my inquiries regarding the present state of the different provinces of Persia, Arabia, Affghanistan, Tartary, and even China, I have always been able to find a person in this city that was either a native of, or had visited, the country regarding which I desired information."

Photographic delineations of the numerous Peoples and Tribes frequenting—

> "(This) Bombay's wealthy isle and harbour fam'd;
> Supine beneath the shade of cocoa groves"—

have long been desiderata both among the students of Geography and Ethnography, and the lovers of Art, notwithstanding partial attempts to supply them made by various local amateurs. The present endeavour to meet the wants of the public in this matter will, it is hoped, meet with indulgence and acceptance. The Collection of Negatives procured for the present work was made with great labour, and in many instances with no little persuasion addressed to the scrupulous personages, whose effigies have been successfully delineated by the solar ray.

For most of the Letterpress Descriptions the Editor is indebted to friends in India, of whom he would venture to name two in particular, the Rev. Dr. Wilson, F.R.S., Honorary President of the Bombay Branch of the Royal Asiatic Society; and the Hon. Alex. Kinloch Forbes, one of the judges of Her Majesty's High Court of Judicature in the Bombay Presidency.

The Series of Photographs will be comprised in Three Volumes, the First Volume embracing Natives of Gujarât, Kutch, and Kâthiawâr; the Second, those of the Maratha Country; and the Third, a Miscellaneous Collection, not properly admissible under the headings of the two first Books.

It will, perhaps, be remarked, as a peculiarity in this Volume, that two different modes of spelling Indian names and words occur in it. In explanation of this seeming inconsistency, the Editor would beg of the reader to remember that the descriptive portion of the work is composed principally of contributed articles, and that different Oriental writers adopt different modes of spelling. Dr. Wilson's contributions embrace the more correct, and to scholars of Asiatic languages perhaps the more acceptable form. In the other articles, especially those which contain extracts from the "Râs Mâlâ," the more popular form adopted by Mr. Forbes has been adhered to.

General Remarks

ON THE

RACES AND TRIBES OF INDIA.

AMONG the Hindus who form the bulk of both the permanent and transient population of Bombay there are, with many varieties, at least two Japhetan or Caucasian races, considerably distant from one another—the darker and the lighter; and a Hamite race, represented by the Mahars and Pariahs, now much degraded, and others of a similar status.

The darker races are those which have been longest in India. Their religion, generally speaking, is the same now as that of the lighter race—the Bráhmanical. All their peoples or tribes, however, preserve traces of an earlier corruption of religion. They are exceedingly addicted to the worship of demons, embodied often in shapeless stones, bedaubed or besmeared with red lead (the symbol of blood), which is considered pleasing to them; to the veneration of the ghosts of their own ancestors and deceased acquaintances; and to the worship of the spirits of the wild beasts which traverse the forests in which they not unfrequently reside. Small bodies of them in certain districts, as in the case of the Wáralis of the Northern Konkan, stand altogether aloof from Bráhmanism. Certain classes of them, like the Bhills and Gonds, are, on account of their unsettled state of life, denominated the WILD TRIBES. The darker race, inhabiting towns and villages, are generally the CULTIVATORS and lower ARTIZANS of the country. Those of them who systematically lead an erratic life, though to some extent pursuing industrial occupations, are called the WANDERING TRIBES. Those of them who, like the Pariahs, are settled in distinct localities, but are not permitted by the Hindu system to live within the walls of villages and towns, may be denominated the DEGRADED TRIBES. Of the latter class considerable numbers are rising in importance in the Indian community.

The FAIRER RACE OF THE HINDUS has generally for the last three thousand years had civil and religious dominion over the darker races, among whom it still maintains its religious authority. Its history is remarkably interesting, though by no means satisfactory either in a religious or philanthropic point of view. It possesses a curious but interesting literature, portions of which are nearly as ancient as the books of Moses. It is intimately connected with the European nations, as proved by the affinities of language; its ancient tongue, the Sanskrit as it has been called, having many striking agreements with the Greek, Latin, German, English, and other languages. Its original seat, shortly after the flood, appears to have been a district of highland country, lying between the eastern portions of the rivers Oxus and Jaxartes, and called in the ancient writings of the Pársís *Airya-Vaejo*, or the Pure Airya, their original paradise. The denomination of the race, from the mountainous locality now mentioned, was that of the *A´ryas* (the Ariani of the Greeks), or the people of A´rya. The A´ryas extended their migrations and settlements to the south and west, particularly to the south. Exterior to India, they possessed several districts of country, which are mentioned in the first chapter of the ancient law book of the Pársís, called the Vandidád. By the Khaibar and Bolan and Himálayan Passes they reached the banks of the various affluents of the Indus about sixteen or seventeen hundred years before the Christian era; and then formed their settlements in the land of the Panchanada, or Five Rivers, called by us the Panjáb, fighting against and subduing the races already darker in their skins than themselves, by whom they had been preceded. In the Panjáb, their poets, some three thousand years ago, often in forgetfulness of the great Creator and upholder of heaven and earth, sang religious songs and hymns, hundreds of which are still in existence (forming the Védas), to the objects and agencies observed by them in the firmament above and the earth below, the principal objects of their worship being their imaginary gods of light. Though then principally a pastoral and agricultural, they were also a military people, considerably advanced in the arts of civilised life, in which they were certainly superior to the blacker peoples who had got to India before them. They gradually spread to the south and south-east, going by the former course along the banks of the Indus, and by the navigation of that great river to its mouths, reaching the ocean. Extending by the latter course, they reached the fertile country lying between the upper Ganges and the Yamuná. Here, before spreading further over the country, they had long their principal settlements; and here their religious and civil polity were developed. They gradually divided themselves into three classes, or castes, according to the occupations required by the particular circumstances of their community—that of the priest, or *Bráhman;* that of the ruler, or warrior, the *Kshatriya;* and that of the cattle-keeper, the field cultivator, and the merchant, the *Vaishya.* The peoples whom they enslaved they called *Shúdras*, from a tribe of the name of Sudra, early conquered by them on the banks of the Indus. To all artizans they ultimately gave a rank inferior to that of Shúdras; and this with little appreciation of labour, skilled or unskilled. The distinctions now referred to still exist among the Hindus, though with certain modifications; while multitudes of other distinctions, embraced in the laws of caste, have been added to them. The Bráhman, in religion and rank, is still at the head of Hindu society, holding, however, at the same time, that the classes intermediate between him and the Shúdra have mostly disappeared.

The Indians, composed, then, as they really are, of different tribes, have great differences in their physiognomy, by which it is not difficult for near observers to recognise them. It is not difficult even for strangers to distinguish them from the people of other tribes, when certain marks which they bear on their persons are attended to. The people who are seen with bedaubments and spots and lines, horizontal and vertical, on their foreheads, and sometimes on their arms and breasts, and with the lower portions of their heads shaven, and a tuft of hair on their crowns, are all Hindus. The spots and lines on their brows are the symbols of their sects and of their castes. They have so many gods, that, despairing to do justice to them all, they choose a favourite one, and set themselves to wearing his marks; and they have so many divisions of class and rank among themselves, that they adopt artificial signs of these classes and ranks. By the tuft on the crown of their heads they distinguish themselves from all other religionists. It is called the *shendi.* They very seldom wear trowsers or breeches. Such of them as do this (except when riding) belong to the lower classes. The higher classes among them wear what is called a *dhotar*, a "washable cloth," which, going round their loins, is suspended in front. These higher classes also, when not Bráhmans, or priests, often wear long stockings, imported from Europe.

The people who are seen with a fairish complexion, with hard and sloping turbans, with their outer vestment like a neckless shirt above their clothes, with wide trousers, with European shoes, or shoes pointed like a curled horn, are Parsis, or Zoroastrians. They all have an inner as well as an outer shirt. It is called their *sadar*, and is viewed by them as a coat of mail, preserving them from the arrows and darts of the devil, who, according to many of them, divides the sovereignty of the universe with God. It is pulled together round their loins by a sacred cincture called the *kusti*, by which they consider themselves bound over to the rites and ordinances which they ascribe to Zoroaster. The Pársís, as merchants, shipbuilders, contractors, and so forth, are the most enterprising natives of India.

Most of the people of India who are not Hindus or Pársís are Muhammadans. They are the descendants of the conquerors of India who preceded the European nations, and who came from the countries lying to the north of India, and of numerous converts—such as Mehmans, Khojahs, and Boharas—made by them from among the Hindus. Their costumes are of very varied form.

The Converts from the natives, made by the Portuguese to Roman Catholicism, have generally adopted, though in a spare form, the European dress. The Converts to Protestantism from all classes of the natives, in the main preserve, with some slight modifications, their original dress, abandoning, however, all the marks and emblems of the religion which they have forsaken. Their object in keeping pretty near their original costume is that of showing their countrymen that religion does not consist in food and apparel.

The Bene-Israel—for in their wide dispersions they, too, have reached India—are distinguished by their wearing a lock of hair above each of their ears. Their dress is like that of the Mercantile Muhammadans.

The CHINESE are easily distinguished by the small opening of their eyes, by their high cheek-bones and flat cheeks, by their thin beards, by their long cues or hair-tails, by their open breasts, by their wide jackets, commodious trowsers, and clog-looking shoes. Their long cues are an exaggeration of the *shendi*, introduced into their native country by the propagation there of the Buddhist religion, which originated in India. The other mysteries of their dress and clothing we profess not to be able to expound, though the following lines of the poet Cowper occur to us:—

"Once on a time, an Emperor, a wise man,
No matter where, in China or Japan,
Decreed that whosoever should offend
Against the well-known duties of a friend,
Convicted once, should ever after wear
But half a coat and show his bosom bare,
The punishment importing this, no doubt,
That all was naught within, and all found out."

The liberty and ease of dress which they enjoy are not, however, to be despised and ridiculed.

The MALAYS somewhat resemble the Chinese, being, like them, of the race of Ham. To use a Hibernian bull (or as we should say in India a *bhul*, a happy blunder), they are something like white Negroes. Some think that the Psalmist, when he realised Kush, or Ethiopia, stretching forth her hands unto God, had both an African and Asiatic extension in view. It is the Asiatic Ethiopia which is referred to in Gen. ii. 13. By religion the Malays are Muhammadans.

The ARABS have very sharp, intelligent countenances, and often high foreheads and long faces. When in their proper costumes they wear a *Kafieh*, or handkerchief, tied round their brow, and flowing over their shoulders. Their outer garment is a capacious cloak. One of the most celebrated anatomists of France speaks of their skulls as the best developed of the human race.

The PERSIANS wear long cylindrical sheepskin caps, with an opening at the side on the top. The sleeves of their outer vestment, have a slit extending to the elbow, and so their arms are bared when raised for action, illustrating to us the figure of God's making bare His holy arm in the sight of the nations. They are a little taller and fairer than the Pársís. They belong, generally speaking, to the Moghal race.

The blackest people frequenting the shores of India are AFRICANS. There are, however, great varieties of shade and form among them. Those of them who, under the names of SIDIS, HABSHIS, and NEGROES, present themselves to view, are a laborious, intelligent, and kindhearted people.

The peculiarities of other peoples to be seen in Bombay will be alluded to in the respective descriptions which are given of them in the progress of this work.

J. W.

OWDICH BRAHMINS.

(No. 1.)

A GREATER variety of Bráhmins is found in Gujarát than in any other province in India. In the current lists no fewer than eighty-four castes of them are specified. These, too, have their own subdivisions, as in the case of the Owdich (so-called from Oude), of whom there are three sections refraining from intermarriage with one another—the Owdich of Sihor, the Tolikyá Owdich, and the Sidhapur Owdich. They are sometimes called the Sahasra Owdich (or the Owdich of the thousand), from the number of individual families who are said to have been attracted to Gujarát from the north of India by King Mulráj, reigning at Anhilvadá Pattan, upwards of 900 years ago. Though they are a pretty numerous body, they have not the standing in the country of some other classes of Bráhmins. Considerable numbers of them are employed as clerks, and not a few of them (especially in the opulent city of Bombay) are procurers of water for the higher classes of native families, who contract no defilement from receiving it at their hands. Some of them, from acting as priests to Mochis and Dirjis (shoemakers and tailors), are called Mochigors, Dirjigors, &c. When they first settled in Gujarát large endowments in land were conferred upon them; but these have been mostly all resumed by the native princes. They are worshippers of Shiva, and generally wear, especially when they wish to be thought to be in a state of purity, the horizontal sectarial marks of that deity. The Shrimáli Bráhmins of Márwár will not take water at their hands, from doubts entertained about their strictness in observing the rules of caste. Great numbers of them go about as Bhikshaks, or mendicants; but this is not reckoned a matter of humiliation to them, as the begging of alms is, by Hindu legislation, an inalienable privilege of the priestly caste. Manu, the legislator, orders the Bráhmin to salute the prince with outspread hands and palms, in the expectation of his getting a reward for his politeness. The causes which led to the subdivisions referred to are thus explained by the author of "Râs Mâlâ":—

"Mool Râj Solunkhee reigned at Unhilpoor, in Goozerat, from 942 to 997 of the Christian era. As the time of his death approached he retired, for the purpose of religious purification, to the holy city of Sidhpoor, on the banks of the Suruswutee river, near his capital. But personal austerities alone, he had been taught, were not sufficient. 'Fasting, vows, bathing, pilgrimages, and penances, when ratified by Bráhmins, are fruitful, not otherwise.' Mool Râj, therefore, prepared, as the scripture of the Owdich caste relates, 'for the reception of holy Bráhmins, with their families, whom he brought, by his intreaties, from the mountains of the north, or from good places of pilgrimage near founts of water, or in the forest. The sons of the sages, well skilled in the Veds, married, youthful, worthy to be served, agreed to repair to the banks of the Virgin river. One hundred and five came from where the Yumona mingles with the Ganges, a hundred readers of the Sâm Ved came from Chyuwun Ashrum, two hundred from Kunyacoobj, one hundred bright as the sun from Benares, two hundred and seventy-two from Kooroo-Kshetra, one hundred from Gungâdwâr, one hundred from Naimeech Arunyâ. A further hundred and thirty-two the King sent for from Kooroo-Kshetra. The smoke of their sacrifices ascended in clouds into the sky.' Mool Râj is said to have conferred upon these Bráhmins lands in the neighbourhood of Sidhpoor, and also to have presented them with the town of Seehore, near Gogo, in the peninsula, and with several villages in the vicinity of both these places. A party of six priests for a long time refused the King's gifts, even after their friends had accepted them, but was at length prevailed upon to receive lands in Cambay and twelve adjacent villages. From the places of their residence the Owdich Bráhmins subsequently assumed the names of Sidhpooreâ and Seehoreeâ Owdich. The party who continued to refuse the gifts of Mool Râj formed a separate caste, called Tolukeeâ Owdich. Since that time, some members of the caste falling into poverty, and being compelled to accept the office of family priest to cobblers, tailors, minstrels, and others, and even to Koolees, have been excommunicated, and have formed so many further subdivisions. Others settling in the city of Surat, or passing into the countries of Kutch, Wagur, or Marwar, and there gradually adopting distinct customs from those authorised at home, have separated from the main body of the caste, and assumed such local names as that of Marwar Owdich Bráhmins."*

In the background of our picture we have a glimpse of the well-known Temple of Shiva, at Walkeshwar, Malabar Hill, Bombay.

* *Vide* "Râs Mâlâ;" or, Hindoo Annals of the Province of Goozerat, in Western India. By Alexander Kinloch Forbes, of the Hon. East India Company's Civil Service. With Illustrations, principally architectural, from drawings by the Author. In two vols. London: Richardson Brothers, 23, Cornhill. 1856. Vol. I., pp. 62—5. Vol II., p. 332.

Oriental Races and Tribes.

Nº 1.

GWDICH BRÁHMINS.

NAGUR BRAHMINS.

(No. 2.)

BRAHMINS will usually eat together, though they decline intermarriages. There is, however, one caste of Brahmins in Goozerat, the Nâgur, which will not even eat with another caste. The original seat of the Nâgur Bráhmins in Goozerat was Wurnuggur, one of the oldest cities in the province. It is said that Veesul Dev Chohân, King of Ujmer, invaded Goozerat in the eleventh century, and, holding possession for a time of part of the province, founded there the city of Veesulnuggur. At this time he caused a sacrifice to be performed which was attended by many Wurnuggur Bráhmins. These refused to receive alms from the King, but Veesul Dev, resorting to a stratagem, forced upon some of them the acceptance of grants of land. They were excommunicated by the body of the caste, and founded the Veesulnuggur Nâgur sect. Similar occurrences at Sâtod and other places produced the Sâtodrâ, the Cheetrodâ, the Prushunorâ, and the Krushunorâ Nâgur Bráhmins. Of this caste there is a division called "Bârud," composed of persons who, finding themselves unable to procure a wife in their own caste, have taken one from another. They are much despised after such a marriage, and compelled to quit their native place; but the sect continues to increase. The Bârud women, contrary to ordinary practice, are permitted to remarry in case they lose their husbands.*

"Bráhmins frequently consider it necessary that they should observe practices of peculiar difficulty, in order to maintain their superiority over the other castes. Of these the most strict is an observance of the Nágur Bráhmins, called 'Nuven,' or 'purity in regard to food.' The Bráhmin having bathed, dresses himself in silk or woollen clothes; or if he require to use cotton garments, these must be dipped in water, wrung out, and dried in some place where nothing impure can touch them. Thus habited, he sits down to dinner, but he must preserve himself from numerous accidents which would render him impure, and compel him to desist from his meal. If he touch an earthen vessel he is defiled, unless the vessel have never contained water. The touch of a piece of cotton cloth, or of a piece of leather or paper, which he may accidentally have sat down upon, renders him impure; but if Hindoo letters have been written on the paper they preserve him from defilement, because they represent 'Suruswutee.' If, however, letters be written on cloth or leather, these remain impure. Thus if the Geeta, or any other portion of Scripture, be required for use at the time, it must be bound with silk, and not with cotton; leather must be avoided, and instead of common paste of flour and water, the binder must employ paste of pounded tamarind seed. A printed book will not answer the Bráhmin's purpose, because printing-ink contains impure matter. Some think that the touch of deer-skin or tiger-skin does not defile. Raw cotton does not render the Bráhmin impure, but if it have been twisted for the wick of a lamp, by a person not in the state of 'Nuven,' it does; and again, if it have been dipped in oil or clarified butter it does not. Bones defile, but women's ivory armlets do not, except in those parts of the country where they are not usually worn, and then they do. The touch of a child of the same caste who has not learned how to eat grain does not defile, but if the child have eaten grain it does. The touch of a donkey, a dog, or a pig, defiles; some say that the touch of a cat also defiles; others are inclined to think that it does not, because, in truth, it is not easy to keep the cat out. If a Bráhmin who is in 'Nuven' be eating, or if he have risen from eating, the touch of his person defiles another Bráhmin who is in 'Nuven,' but has not begun his dinner."†

The Nâgur Bráhmins form a numerous and influential class both in Goozerat and in Bombay, and occupy positions of trust and responsibility in mercantile and Government offices. They are generally considered men of talent and ability. In our group we have Vukeels (native advocates), schoolmasters, an accountant, bill and share brokers, and last, not least, a poet of some celebrity amongst the Goozeratee population of Bombay.

Our group of Nâgur Bráhmins presents, it will be observed, a great variety of head-dress, ranging from the full white turban of Katiawar, and the rounded one of Ahmedabad, to the half-Mogulised costume of Surat, and the broad, flat head-dress which the Nâgur resident in Bombay sometimes adopts from the Bráhmins of the Deccan.

* *Vide* "Râs Mâlâ." Vol. II., p. 233.

† *Vide* "Râs Mâlâ." Vol. II., pp. 258-9.

Nº 2.
NAGUR BRÁHMINS.

NAGAR BRAHMAN WOMEN.

(No. 3.)

THE word *nágar* is the adjective form of *nagar*, a city. It is applied to a class of Bráhmans in Goozerat, which again has six divisions—the Vadnagar, Visalnagar, Sathodra, Prashnora, Krishnora, and Chitrodá, so named from the villages in which they first settled when they established themselves in the province. They are a very intelligent people, and large numbers of them are devoted to secular employment, particularly in connexion with the agencies of the different native chiefs of Kathiáwár. The duties and services which they exact of their females are the same as those practised by Bráhman females in general—such as the management of the younger children, cooking, and keeping the house clean and orderly. They have made a commencement of female education in a few of their families, and in schools lately established at Bhávanagar, Surat, and Ahmadabad. The parties represented in our photograph are but young in years. They have on the graceful and modest costume worn by the better classes of their caste, with a moderate supply of ornaments—noselets, earrings, necklaces, bracelets, anklets, and toelets. Though not allowed to learn or repeat any of the sacred mantras or verses of the Védas, or to touch the idols in their houses or temples, the Bráhmanis make offerings to the gods through the hands of the officiating priests, take and fulfil vows, perform perambulation round sacred trees and images, listen to the recitation of the Puránas and other legendary works, tend the sacred tulasi plant *(Ocymum sanctum)*, make ready wicks for lamps to enlighten them on the path to heaven, prepare pigments for family and personal use, and draw ornamental figures at their thresholds and on the floors of their houses. They never go to market to make purchases, or carry loads or bundles. Neither do they ride on horseback, as is sometimes done by the Bráhmanis of the Dakhan. Their social morality is well guarded by their families. They seldom leave their houses, even for exercise, though they occasionally exchange visits with their female friends.

It will be seen on a microscopic examination of the picture that, in addition to the various ornaments already enumerated, the lady on the left is adorned with what we suppose would be termed a toothlet—a gold button screwed on to a front tooth, which is bored to receive it. This is a species of ornament peculiar, we were told, to this class of Hindu women. We certainly never remember to have seen it on the person of any other female.

J. W.

No 8.

NAGAR BRÁHMIN WOMEN.

VALLABHÁCHÁRYA MAHÁRÁJAS.

(No. 4.)

VALLABHA was the son of a Bráhman of Telingána, who flourished towards the end of the fifteenth and the beginning of the sixteenth century of the Christian era. He was patronised by Krishna Déva, King of Vijayanagar; but it was in the north of India that he came into special notice as an A'chárya, or religious teacher. He became a devotee of the god Krishna, who, though a king, was soon viewed by the Hindus as the personification of love and lust; and of this god, either he himself, or his early followers acting for him, pretended that he was an incarnation. He became the founder of a sect, the principles of which may be learned from the following notices: "Amongst other articles of the new creed, Vallabha introduced one which is rather singular for a Hindu religious innovator or reformer: He taught that privation formed no part of sanctity, and that it was the duty of the teacher and his disciples to worship their deity, not in nudity and hunger, but in costly apparel and choice food; not in solitude and mortification, but in the pleasures of society and the enjoyment of the world. The *Gosains*, or teachers, are almost all family men, as was the founder Vallabha; for, after he had taken off the restrictions of the monastic order to which he originally belonged, he married, by the particular order, it is said, of his new god. The Gosains are always clothed with the best raiment, and fed with the daintiest viands by their followers, over whom they have unlimited influence."—("Essays on the Hindu Religion," by Professor H. H. Wilson.) "The sect of Vallabhácharya is a new sect, inasmuch as it has selected the god Krishna in one of his aspects—that of his adolescence—and raised him to supremacy in that aspect. It is a new sect, in as far as it has established the *Pushti-Márya*, or way of enjoyment in a natural and carnal sense. The god Krishna is worshipped by its members in the form of images, and in the form of the persons of their Gurus, the so-called Mahárájahs."—(Examination of Rev. Dr. John Wilson before the Supreme Court of Bombay, 8th Feb., 1862.) These Gurus, or Mahárájas (for they have usurped a royal title) comprehend all the descendants of Vallabha. They are viewed by a great many of their followers as incarnations of the head of Krishna, and as intermediate between Krishna and his worshippers. In their alleged religious authorities it is said, "We should regard our Guru as God; for if God get angry, the Guru Déva is able to save from the effects of God's anger; whereas, if the Guru is displeased, nobody is able to save from the effects of the Guru's displeasure." To Krishna, through the Mahárájas, the Vallabhácháryas dedicate their body, soul, and property (*tan*, *man*, and *dhan*), and large numbers of them have allowed them access to their wives and daughters. The practice of gross immorality (with the supposed sanction of religion) has been the consequence. A calm reprobation of this immorality by Karsandas Muljí, the enlightened and able editor of a native paper advocating reform, lately brought a prosecution upon him for libel, which occupied the attention of the Supreme Court of Bombay for twenty-four days, but which issued in his justification. On this occasion the prosecutor was a Maháráj, named Jadunathji, who was himself accused of perjury, in denying his own loathsome practices, by both the judges, Sir M. Sausse and Sir J. Arnould. The disclosures made in the case were of a most extraordinary character—the most astounding, in some respects, perhaps, ever made in a court of justice. It was long before the prosecution was commenced that the photograph, given in this volume, of five of the Mahárájas, was made. A peculiar interest is to be attached to it, as will be readily understood from the preceding notices. It will be observed that the parties whom it represents wear their hair as women, and have such ornaments on their persons, extending to their toes, as in India are worn only by the female sex. Their object in this is to characterise themselves as *Gopis* (herdswomen devoted to Krishna), and to indicate that women united to them are joined only to the god himself. The system of faith and practice with which the Vallabhácháryas are connected was warmly and powerfully reprobated by the Bombay judges, especially by Sir J. Arnould. It is professed by several hundred thousands of Hindus in the north-west of India; but it is now attacked by a hopeful body of determined reformers, including several individuals of great influence in the native community. In the meantime the Mahárájas (of whom seven or eight—a tithe of the whole fraternity—were wont to be in Bombay) have, with a single exception, left the city. Its streets are certainly not less clean and safe since they have been forsaken by these "Brahminy Bulls." For anything we know to the contrary, the five whose shadows were caught before their departure may be better than their neighbours. Their names (beginning with that of him on the left hand of the spectator) are Gopkeshjí, Jivanjí, Maganlal, Gokuládhísh, and Chimanjí.

We are indebted to Dr. Narrain Dajee, a medical practitioner in Bombay, and an accomplished photographer, for the original photograph, or negative, from which our picture is made.

J. W.

No. 4.

WALLABHÁCHÁRYA MAHÁRÁJAS.

RAJPOOTS.

(No. 5.)

"IT is stated in the 'Bhâgwut Poorân' that Mureechee Reeshee, the son of Brumhâ, had a son, Kusyup, whose son, Soorya (the sun), or Veevuswân, became a Kshutruya. Mureechee's brother, Utree, had also a son named Som, or Chundra (names of the moon), and he, too, was a warrior. The great majority of the Rajpoot clans deduce their descent from either Soorya, or Chundra. In the commentary on a Sanskrit work called 'Rutun Kosh,' it is said that the first of the Kshutruya race was Munoo, and that from him sprung thirty-six tribes, of whom some acquired surnames by valiant exploits, some attained the rank of kings, others fell to that of cultivators, or even became lost in the Shúdra caste. Chund Bhârot states that when the sages dwelt on Mount Aboo, and were annoyed by the Usoors, or demons, Wushist, one of their number, created from a sacrificial pit of fire four Kshutruyas—Pureehâr, Solunkhee, Purmâr, and Chohân. From these sprung the thirty-six Rajpoot clans, which he thus enumerates:—

"The Sun, the Moon, the Jâduv[1] races,
Kukoosth, Purmâr, and Tonwur,
Châhoowân,[2] Châlook,[3]
Chind,[4] Silar, Abheewur,
Doyamutt,[5] Mukwan,[6]
Gurooâ, Gohill, Gahiloot,
Châpotkut,[7] Pureehâr,
Râv Râthor the angry,
Deorâ, Thânk, Sindhuv, Unig,
Yotik, Prutheehâr, Dudheekuth,
Kârutpâl, Kotpâl, Hoon,
Hureetuth, Gor, Kumâd, Jutt,
Dhyânpâluk, Nikoombh, great,
Rajpâl, lords of earth,
Kâluchur, last of all.
I have named the thirty-six races.

"The common version now given by bards is that five Rajpoots—Purmâr, Râthor, Jâduv, Chahoowân, and Solunkhee—sprang from the fire-pit, and that from these descend ninety-nine clans. The Rajpoot tribes still maintain that they are true Kshutruyas, though the Bráhmins deny that the warrior caste has any longer an existence. The reason is to be found in the affected purity, as regards food and other matters, which has crept upon the Bráhmins, and in the compulsory marriage of Rajpoot ladies with the Mohummedan princes. The Kshutruya caste is now no longer considered by other Hindoos to be next in rank to the Bráhmin; its place has been usurped by the Wâneeâs, a branch of the Vaíshya caste, who will not even drink water with Rajpoots, and 'Bráhmin-Wâneeâ' is now a synonymous expression for 'oojulee-wustee,' or high-caste population. The Rajpoots use animal food and spirituous liquor, both unclean in the last degree to their puritanic neighbours, and are scrupulous in the observance of only two rules—those which prohibit the slaughter of cows, and the re-marriage of widows. The clans are not forbidden to eat together or to intermarry, and cannot be said in these respects to form different castes.

"In times of peace and ease the Rajpoot leads an indolent and monotonous life. It is some time, usually after sunrise, before he bestirs himself, and begins to call for his hookah; after smoking, he enjoys the luxury of tea or coffee, and commences his toilet and ablutions, which dispose of a considerable part of the morning. It is soon breakfast time, and after breakfast the hookah is again in requisition, with but few intervals of conversation, until noon. The time has now arrived for a siesta, which lasts until about three in the

[1] The Jâduv, or Yâduv, to which the Râs of Soreth belonged.

[2] Chohân. [3] Solunkhee. [4] Chundel. [5] Dâheemâ. [6] Mukwanâ, or Jhâlâ. [7] Chowra.

afternoon. At this hour the chief gets up again, washes his hands and face, and prepares for the great business of the day—the distribution of the red cup, kusoombâ, or opium. He calls together his friends into the public hall, or perhaps retires with them to a garden-house. Opium is produced, which is pounded in a brass vessel and mixed with water; it is then strained into a dish with a spout, from which it is poured into the chief's hand. One after the other the guests now come up, each protesting that kusoombâ is wholly repugnant to his taste, and very injurious to his health, but after a little pressing, first one and then another touches the chief's hand in two or three places, muttering the names of Devs, friends or others, and drains the draught. Each, after drinking, washes the chief's hand in a dish of water which a servant offers, and wipes it dry with his own scarf; he then makes way for his neighbour. After this refreshment the chief and his guests sit down in the public hall, and amuse themselves with chess, draughts, or games of chance; or perhaps dancing-girls are called in to exhibit their monotonous measures, or musicians and singers, or the never-failing favourites—the Bhâts and Châruns. At sunset the torch-bearers appear, and supply the chamber with light; upon which all those who are seated therein rise and make obeisance towards the chieftain's cushion. They resume their seats, and playing and singing, dancing, story-telling, go on as before. At about eight the chief rises to retire to his dinner and his hookah, and the party is broken up.

"The Rajpoot chief has always several ladies, each of whom is maintained in a separate suite of apartments. He dines and spends the evening alternately in the apartments of each of the ladies, who, with her attendants, prepares dinner for him, and waits upon him while he eats it, waving the punkah or fan behind him, and entertaining him with her remarks, which, if report speak true (for no stranger is admissible on such occasions), frequently constitute a pretty severe curtain lecture.*

Bombay was visited last year by two of the Rajpoot chiefs of Goozerat, who, with their attendant noblemen, form the subject of our picture.

Muhârâjâ Jowan Singh, Rajah of Eedur, the central figure in our group, is the head of the Rhâtor clan—the present Rajah of Marwar being the son of his father's younger brother. The principality of Eedur is in the hilly country in the north of Goozerat.

This chief is tributary to the Guikowar, and his lands are not included in the British territory. There are many Rajpoot chiefs, however, in British Goozerat, commonly known by the name of Talookdars. Their affairs have generally fallen into confusion from causes which will be hinted at in our description of the Wâneeâ caste; and the newly-revived Legislature of Bombay was employed during its first Session in discussing the provisions of an Encumbered Estates Bill, intended to remedy the disadvantages under which they have fallen.

* *Vide* "Ras Mâlâ," Vol. II., pp. 233, 235, 261, 262.

No 5.

RAJPOOTS.

BHÂTS.

(No. 6.)

CLOSELY connected with the Rajpoots are the Bards, the Bhâts, and the Châruns. Of their origin nothing is known, but they assert themselves to have sprung from Muha Dev or Shiva. They are in some places cultivators, in others bankers, but their more legitimate occupations are those of acting as securities for the performance of engagements, and of recording the genealogies of their Rajpoot clients.

"During the anarchy which has more or less prevailed in Goozerat from the time when the dynasty of Unhilpoor was overthrown by the Mohummedans to the time when, under British influence, the settlement was effected which we have described, the security of a bard was one of the few available means of ensuring the performance of both political engagements and private agreements, and of providing for the safe transaction of commercial operations. Whether the paramount power sought a guarantee from the half-independent principalities for the payment of their tribute, or a private individual desired assurance of oblivion and personal safety from the chief whom he had offended—whether the money-lender looked for a pledge of repayment, or the merchant for the safe transit of his goods through a country infested with robbers—the bard was alike resorted to as the only person whose security could be accepted without danger. As the descendant and favourite of the gods, his person was sacred in the eyes of men who reverenced but little else, and he had at his command means of extorting compliance with his demands which were seldom used in vain. These were the rites of 'Trâgâ' and 'Dhurnâ,' which consisted—the former, in the shedding by the bard of the blood of himself, or of some member of his family, and the calling down upon the offender whose obstinacy necessitated the sacrifice the vengeance of heaven; and the latter in placing around the dwelling of the recusant a cordon of bards, who fasted, and compelled the inhabitants of the house also to fast, until their demands were complied with. It was not until the establishment of British supremacy rendered the performance of these barbarous rites impossible that the custom of employing bardic security fell into disuse.

"In his heraldic and poetical capacity, however, it is that the bard has been longest and most favourably distinguished. When the rainy season closes, and travelling becomes practicable, the bard sets off on his yearly tour from his residence in the 'Bhâtwârâ' of some city or town. One by one he visits each of the Rajpoot chiefs who are his patrons, and from whom he has received portions of land, or annual grants of money, timing his arrival, if possible, to suit occasions of marriage, or other domestic festivals. After he has received the usual courtesies, he produces the 'Wye'—a book written in his own crabbed hieroglyphics, or in those of his father's, which contains the descent of the house, if the chief be the 'Teelâyut,' or head of the family, from the founder of the tribe; if he be a 'Phutâyo,' or cadet, from the immediate ancestor of the branch, interspersed with many a verse or ballad, the 'dark sayings' contained in which are chanted forth in musical cadence to a delighted audience, and are then orally interpreted by the bard, with many an illustrative anecdote or tale. The 'Wye' is not, however, merely a source for the gratification of family pride or even of love of song. It is also a record of authority by which questions of consanguinity are determined, when marriage is on the tapis, and disputes relating to the division of ancestral property are decided, intricate as these last necessarily are, from the practice of polygamy, and the rule that all the sons of a family are entitled to a share. It is the duty of the bard at each periodical visit to register the births, marriages, and deaths which have taken place in the family since his last circuit, as well as to chronicle all the other events worthy of remark which have occurred to affect the fortunes of his patron; nor have we ever heard even a doubt suggested regarding the accurate, much less the honest, fulfilment of this duty by the bard.

"The manners of the bardic tribe are very similar to those of their Rajpoot clients; their dress is nearly the same, but the bard seldom appears without the 'Kutâr,' or dagger, a representation of which is scrawled beside his signature, and often rudely engraved upon his monumental stone, in evidence of his death in the sacred duty of 'Trâgâ.' The heraldic occupation is hereditary, and as the bard goes forth on his annual circuits, attended not only by his servants and retinue (the females only being left at home), but also by his sons, the latter have numerous opportunities of becoming acquainted with the history of their patrons, and of learning beside the funeral monuments of the race, all that traditionary lore which forms their ancestral wealth."*

* Râs Mâlâ, Vol. II., pp. 262—5.

Oriental Races and Tribes.

Nº 6.
BHÂTS.

KHUWÂS AND GOLÂS.

(No. 7.)

SLAVERY—though not now a recognised institution in India—has left traces over many parts of the country of its existence at no very distant period. This is specially the case in Katheawar and Kutch, where we have a people who are only known there and elsewhere by names which imply a condition of slavery, and who form amongst themselves a distinct portion of the varied population of those provinces. These are the Golâs, or, as they are sometimes called, Khuwâs, the latter term merely representing those who had attained to some better position in the household of their masters than that ordinarily assigned to the members of their community. Descendants of women who had been purchased as slaves, these people still regard themselves as "hereditary slaves," and are perhaps so regarded by a large majority of their neighbours. They are to be found in the household of every chief or man of note in Katheawar and Kutch. They are generally well treated, well fed, and well clothed, rising at times to positions of trust and responsibility. Their costume is usually that of the district in which they may be residing, and they are either Hindoos or Mahomedans, according to the religion of their masters. Those whom we have illustrated were amongst the personal attendants who accompanied the Rajpoot chief of Eidur on his visit to Bombay last year—one of them, the central figure, being a man of some consequence amongst his fellows. Forbes' "Râs Mâlâ" contains the following brief allusion to these people:—

"At the residence of every Rajpoot chief are to be found a number of female servants, either themselves purchased as slaves when young, or the descendants of women who have been thus purchased. They are of all castes, and are frequently even Abyssinians—in Kâtewâr the usual name for them is *Chokree*, in the Myhee Kântâ it is *Wudhârun*. These women are reputed to be of easy virtue, and are hardly ever married at all; but if they are, it is with a member of their own caste. An intrigue with them is considered disgraceful to a member of another class. When a Wudhârun is found to be with child, the Ranee, her mistress, will send for her, and compel her to disclose the name of the father, who, if a wealthy person, is compelled to pay a fine. No fault, however, is imputed to the woman. The children bear the name of Golâ, or, if they have been employed in high situations by the chief, that of Khuwâs. They remain, however, the slaves of the chief, notwithstanding their promotion. On the marriage of a chief's daughter, a certain number of male and female slaves form part of the young lady's dowry. They perform the menial duties of the household, and used sometimes to accompany the corpse of their chief to the funeral pile, and burn themselves thereupon."

No 7.

KHUWÂS AND GOLÂS.

BANIANS, OR WANEEAS.

(Nos. 8, 9, 10, and 11.)

WE have here four pictures, in which Banians, as they are usually called, or Wâneeâs, as they are more correctly styled, are depicted. The first picture represents the Wâneeâ costume of Ahmedabad, in the centre figure, with those of Surat on the right hand, and Gogo and the surrounding country on the left. The second exhibits Wâneeâs from Porebunder, a port on the south-west coast of Káteewár; the third, the same class of people from Damnuggur, in the east of the Peninsula, hardly distinguishable from the two Sonées, or goldsmiths (the right and left figures), by whom they are accompanied; and the fourth, a group of Banian Women. As these people are so intimately related that the one can hardly be considered without the other, we propose to treat of them together; and, at the same time, to show how the necessity arose for the Encumbered Estates enactment, to which we have already alluded in our description of the Rajpoots:—

"In Goozerat and Káteewár Vaishyas are still employed principally in agriculture and commerce. Of the trading classes, the principal are the Wâneeâs, already mentioned, who form eighty-four distinct castes, deriving names principally from districts or towns. These castes are again subdivided, as into right and left hand, or into Dushâ and Veeshâ, names implying degrees of rank, and derived from words signifying ten and twenty. The Wâneeâs are still further divided by religious differences, as into Meshrees, or Vaishnavite Hindoos, and Shrâwuks, or Jains. The genealogists of the Wâneeâs, Jain monks, or bards, as the case may be, derive their descent commonly from some Rajpoot clan. Intermarriage is not allowed where the parties are reputed to be of the same descent. . . .

"Wâneeâs and trading people generally set off early in the morning to have a sight of the Dev in his temple. Some persons entertain a superstitious notion that everything will prosper with them during the day if they behold a particular person's face the first thing in the morning; so they keep their eyes as completely closed as they can, and set off to see this person of good omen. It is very unlucky, they believe, to see a man who has no son, an outcast, a donkey, or a quarrelsome person. Others worship the first thing in the morning the sacred basil, or the holy fig tree. After they have eaten breakfast and chewed betel, they set off to the public market, where they follow their occupation until evening time, when they return home to dinner, paying, perhaps, on their way, a second visit to the temple.

"It is the men's business to make what purchases are necessary for the household in the market, and to keep the accounts. All other domestic duties devolve upon the women.

"The wives of the poorer class of householders rise at three in the morning frequently to grind grain; and are occupied, perhaps, for three hours in preparing as much flour as will last until the third day. When they have no grain to grind they must still rise at the same early hour to milk the cows, churn, and extract clarified butter. At six o'clock, after arranging their costume, they set off with their vessels to the river side, where they bathe and fill water, and then return home. Some women bathe at home, and fetch water afterwards; and rich men's wives have a servant specially for attendance on the bath. When the women return with their water-vessels filled they must set to work to prepare breakfast. The males of the family, when breakfast is ready, sit down in a line at short intervals, and eat; when they rise, the women sit down. Breakfast finished, and the men off to their various duties, the women are busily employed in cleaning the house, the fireplace, the plates and dishes, and other vessels, and in preparing grain for grinding. About three in the afternoon they have a little leisure, which they employ in attending to their children or in combing out their own long hair and oiling it. In the evening they are again busy getting ready lights, preparing dinner, and spreading the beds.

"When a caste entertainment takes place the guests either wash at home, and dress themselves in silk clothes, or, if the distance be considerable, carry their dining dress with them to the house of their host, who provides them with water to bathe in. When they are dressed, the men sit down in two lines outside the entertainer's house, and take their dinner; as soon as they have finished their repast, the women sit down in a similar manner. In some places the women dine at the same time as the men, but at a short distance from them. The persons who prepared the dinner set it before the guests, and dine themselves when the rest have finished. On the west of the Sâbhurmutee River the women dress for dinner in cotton, which practice is the subject of much contemptuous remark among the people of the eastern districts, whose wives wear silk dresses. In some places no person, not even a man of the caste, unless he have bathed and dressed himself in silk, can pass between the two lines of guests at a public feast without defiling the company, and it becomes therefore necessary that the entertainer should procure permission to barricade the street in which he lives. In other parts of the country a person of the same, or of higher caste, may pass without removing his clothes, but he must leave his shoes behind him, and carry his turban in his hand; and, above all, he must be particular not to carry with him a book bound in leather, or any other leathern article. Five or six of the caste are usually stationed on either side of the lines to keep off the dogs—a task in which they are not always successful; and when a dog gets in, his appearance creates quite a scuffle; hands are raised on all sides to drive him away, and it generally ends in his putting his foot into some man's plate, and jumping over him, or else in his rushing between two men, rendering them both impure. The sufferers, however, put up with the affront quietly for the time being, and finish what is in their plates, that they may not be guilty of disrespect to Unn Dev (food personified as a deity), or sometimes they call to the sentinels, who remove their plates, and bring them fresh ones.

"It is, unfortunately, matter of notoriety that, speaking generally, all the cultivators and holders of land in Goozerat are in debt to such an extent, that they have no means of their own of extricating themselves from their difficulties. The creditors are for the most part Goozerat Wâneeâs of the Meshree (Vaishnavite) or Shrâwuk (Jain) classes. A Wâneeo commencing life spends his time partly in a large town, and partly in some remote country village.

He borrows a few rupees at interest in the town, with which he purchases small supplies of clarified butter, oil, molasses, and other such articles, and thus stocks his village shop. The cultivators having no money at hand, barter small quantities of their grain or cotton for as much oil as will keep their evening lamp burning for an hour, or for little supplies of groceries. They are perfectly unaware of the market value of their raw produce, and are quite satisfied that they have made a bargain if the Wâneeo, with a politic show of liberality, throws in a little more of the article he is selling under the name of a bonus. Having collected a sufficient quantity of raw produce, the trader carries it to the town, and sells it there at a favourable rate; and, his capital thus augmented, he returns to the village to commence operations on a larger scale. A cultivator, perhaps, has lost his bullock; the Wâneeo steps forward immediately to lend him money, at interest, to supply his loss. Or, perhaps, the Koonbee is engaged in marrying his child, or in performing the funeral rites of his parent; the trader will advance him money to supply him with the clarified butter, molasses, clothes, or other articles which are indispensable on these occasions, charging for them twice their value. Sometimes the cultivator prefers to make his own purchases in the town, but he must then take the Wâneeo with him to act as broker between him and the town dealer, for he feels that the latter will otherwise charge him anything he pleases; and, besides, he has no money, and cannot borrow it except from the village lender; for the curious feeling in regard to rights, which is so prevalent among the Hindoos, applies here, and the village Wâneeo will consider his property invaded if any other trader propose to deal with his constituents. On these transactions the Wâneeo, of course, gains largely. Sometimes, however, he will say to the cultivator, 'I have no ready money; but if you will tell me what you want, we will go together and purchase it, and it shall be put down to my account.' He takes care, moreover, to hint to his victim what praises he has heard of the liberality of the family, and how necessary it is that their honour should be maintained by a large expenditure on the present occasion. He adds that such celebrations do not happen every day, but only once or twice in a lifetime, that the money will not be thrown away, and that nothing is easier than to make it up again. He will also say, 'I have every confidence in you, and am ready to advance you any sum you wish.' In this way, flattering his pride, he easily plunges him deeply into debt.

"When the occasion for all this extravagant expenditure has passed away, the Wâneeo demands his bond. He tells the cultivator, 'You have so much to pay to the ghee-dealer, so much to the cloth-seller,' and so on; to all of which the cultivator assents The Wâneeo says, 'Now give me my kothulee chorâmun,' meaning a fee for loosening the purse-strings, which must be paid in ready money, for luck, or as a good omen. The cultivator procures one per cent. in ready money from wherever he can, and pays it. He has further, also, to make a present, not only to the person who writes, but also to those who attest the bond. Interest is stipulated for at two per cent. per mensem, or, if the terms are unusually moderate, at one. The bond prepared, the cultivator scrawls beneath it his mark—a rude representation of a plough. When the next crop is ready, and the Government share has been paid, the creditor exerts himself to carry off all that remains. The cultivator, with much intreaty, obtains enough to subsist upon for a short time, and he is credited, on account of the remainder, with whatever the Wâneeo may be pleased to allow him. Sometimes the trader carries off nearly the whole, and when the cultivator talks about a subsistence, says, 'What need you care? when yours is done, you can have as much as you like from my shop.' Thus the cultivator is driven to the Wâneeo's shop for grain to eat, and grain to sow his field with. The terms of lending are, that the borrower shall repay twice the quantity of grain he takes away, when his crop ripens. The next harvest comes round, but now all the grain which is left, after the payment of the Government demands, goes to pay for that which was borrowed last year, and there is nothing left to pay the interest of the bond. This, then, must be added to the principal; and so the bond goes on swelling year by year—the trader (who is well aware of the practice of the courts of justice) taking care to have it periodically renewed, and carefully closing every loop-hole through which his victim might escape.

"The creditor will now probably reside principally in the town, and on his occasional visits to the village he puts up at the house of his debtor, who is obliged to maintain him as long as he remains there. If the Wâneeo have a son to marry, or a pilgrimage to perform, the debtor is obliged to lend him his cart and bullocks, and on such occasions he must also come forward with the usual present. The money-lender has by this time begun to assume a very high tone, and to demand payment, threatening to sell the cultivator's house or his bullocks; in fact, as a villager would say, 'He becomes more oppressive than a raja.'

"In a few years the Wâneeo, having thus made himself the master of numerous cultivators, amasses a large sum of money. He now turns his attention to a higher prey, and seeks to become the creditor of local chiefs and landowners. His first step is to get himself introduced to the chief's man of business, whom he gains over by gifts and promises. This agent accordingly takes the first opportunity of praising the trader in the chief's presence, and intimating his readiness to advance as much money as may be wished for. When occasion arrives, money is accordingly borrowed from the Sowkâr, or Shet (at which dignity the Wâneeo has now arrived), and the man of business prepares a bond and brings it to the landowner for his signature. The chief haggles like a child for a sum of ready money to be presented to him as the price of his affixing his seal, but cares little or nothing about what there is in the bond; never reflecting for a moment that he is likely to be called upon to fulfil his agreement. A few transactions of this kind lead to the inevitable termination The Sowkâr sues in the court of justice; the man of business (who has carefully abstained from keeping any account, lest his own peculations should be exposed) deserts his master in the hour of need. The chief attempts to defend his suit; and while he admits that he has signed the bond, urges that he is not really indebted to one-tenth of the extent asserted. He is informed that he must produce his accounts, in order to prove his defence; and when he states that his agent never kept any, is told further that this is merely a false statement, made because the production of the books called for would prove the validity of the plaintiff's claim. The chief has, of course, no further defence; a decree is therefore passed, and his estate is attached."*

* Râs Mâlâ, Vol. II., pp. 236—248—252—259—261.

Nº 8.

BANIANS OF SURAT, GOGO, AND AHMEDABAD.

No. 9.

BANIANS OF POREBUNDER.

No. 10.

BANIANS AND SONEES OF DAMNUGGUR.

Nº 11.
BANIAN WOMEN.

GHUR-BÁREE (HOUSE-HOLDING) GOSÁEES.

(No. 12.)

OUR present picture exhibits a group of house-holding Gosáees, or Uteets, of whom a considerable number reside at Eedur, Sidhpoor, and other places in Goozerat, and occupy the position of wealthy bankers. The following description of himself and his caste was furnished to us some years ago by a Gosáee, named Vishnoogurjee, and as it is tolerably comprehensive, as well as authentic, we give it in full:—

"I am an inhabitant of Tirhoot, in Nepaul. My father, Oopādya Mohunrám, a Shunkuldweepee Bráhmin, on account of his having no offspring, made a vow at the temple of Chutra-bhooj, in Moozufurpoor, that if he should have two sons he would devote one of them; so I was born soon after, and when I was about five years old my mother had a second son, and my father resolved to consecrate me to the god. The Muhānunt, or high-priest of the temple, cut off the lock of hair that was on my head, and thus became my goroo. He also instructed me. I have since wandered about from one Hindoo sacred place to another, and have visited Káshee, Jwálá-mookhee, Hurdwár, Dwárká, and other shrines. I live at any temple, or 'Ukháro,' which is frequented by naked Gosáees. I have been lately staying at Neelkunt Muhá Dev's, at Ahmedabad, with Heerápuree Muhánunt. Three months ago I left that, and I am now on my way to the temple of Umbâ Bhuwánee. In the rainy season I take shelter anywhere where I can find a person to support me. My occupation is pilgrimage ('Chuktáee'), and I live upon alms. Shree Shunkur (Shiva) is the deity I worship. Before the time of the English Government people of my caste did not marry, for fear of their caste-fellows revenging this breach of rules. Some now marry, but not those who travel about naked, with their hair arranged in a conical form on their heads, which head-dress is called 'Juttá.' When they become house-holders they let down the 'Juttá' and wear clothes, and they must also divest themselves of the copper ear-ornament called 'Moondra.' There are four sects of Uteets, each of which is divided into three branches:—

I. JOSHEE-MUT......	1. Gur branch.	III. BOGHORDUN-MUT...	1. Bun.
	2. Purbut.		2. Orun.
	3. Ságur.		3. Jutee.
II. SINGHEREE-MUT...	1. Pooree.	IV. SA'RDA-MUT.........	1. Jot.
	2. Bhártee.		2. Rāmādutee.
	3. Suruswutee.		3. Dundee.

I am a Gur of the Joshee-mut. The house-holding members of the four sects intermarry, but members of the same branch do not intermarry. If an Uteet take a woman of another caste into his house, she is unclean until she has received the rites of initiation. The naked Gosáees are all of the Bráhmin caste. In many places Uteets are employed as Sepoys; they then, but not otherwise, bear arms, and they generally wear an orange-tawny cloth round their heads instead of a turban. Whatever clothes they wear must be of this colour. They obey a chief called a Mookhee as long as the service lasts. Uteets are not burned on the funeral pyre, but buried in the position in which Hindoos usually sit, with the arms folded, wearing a close-fitting orange-tawny cap and a cloak of the same colour, with a staff, an earthen vessel upon the head, wooden sandals, a wallet, and a drinking gourd. As much salt as can be procured is poured over the body; and if money be forthcoming, Uteets, Sádhoos, Bráhmins, &c., are entertained on the twelfth day after death. Uteets frequently cause themselves to be buried alive in this manner when they believe their death to be near."

A. K. F.

Oriental Races and Tribes.

No. 12.

GHUR-BÁREE (HOUSE-HOLDING) GOSÁEES.

BHATIAS.

(No. 13.)

THE Bhátiás (or Bhátyás) are originally from the country of Bhátiner, between Sindh and Rájputáná. Their first emigrations were to Kutch and Káthiáwár. Multitudes of them are now in Bombay, in which they form a very important portion of its diversified native community, being greatly distinguished for their industry and enterprise. Many of them, too, are found as mercantile agents in the seaports of the Red Sea and Persian Gulf, and even of the coasts of Africa. They reckon themselves to be Kshatriyas, or the descendants of the princely caste; but they are generally viewed by the Bráhmans as only Vaishyas, members of the mercantile body. They wear the tunic, zone, and pendant front-cloth common among the Hindus; but they are at once cognizable by their high and pointed turbans of printed cotton, with bright colours, which, contrasted with the head-dresses of many other classes of natives, give them rather an imposing appearance. Comparatively, they are of a fair complexion. They are devotees of the god Krishna, and followers of the sectarial teacher Vallabhácháryá, the licentious tenets and practices of whom and his descendants have lately met with such a disgusting (but, it is to be hoped, salutary) exposure in the Supreme Court of Bombay, in the celebrated great Mahárúj Libel Case, directed against Karsandás Muljí, whose able pen had been engaged in their reprobation in the *Satya Prakásh*, a Gujarátí newspaper published in Bombay. Having alluded to this fact, it is right for us to mention that a powerful reforming party exists among the Bhátiás, headed by such intelligent and influential men as Messrs. Lakhmidás Khimjí and Mathurádás Lowjí, from whose vigour and decision of character improvements may be expected both in the creed and moral conduct of the people of the tribe. It is to be regretted that education, properly so called, has made but little progress in their community. Almost all the names of the Bhátiás are designations of the god Krishna.

J. W.

No 13.

BHÁTIÁS.

LOWANA WOMEN.

(No. 14.)

LOWANAS, or rather Lohánás (for they derive their designation from the fort of Loha), are a Hindu tribe, originally from the Province of Sindh. Their present head-quarters are in Kutch. Speaking of them as connected with that country, the late Captain James Macmurdo thus describes them in the third volume of the "Transactions of the Bombay Literary Society": "In Kutch they are labourers, cultivate the soil, or speculate in trade. They were for many years Ministers of the Kutch Government; but the principal men having been cruelly put to death by one of the Ráos, the caste, since that time, has declined in consequence and respectability. The Lowánás eat flesh and drink spirits in a public manner. They are of industrious habits, and, being naturally a robust and strong race of men, perform very severe labour. They are, nevertheless, licentious in their manners, and much importance is not attached [by them] to chastity. The Lowánás wear the Bráhmanical string or Jánave [the badge of Kshatriyas and Vaishyas, as well as of Bráhmans]. Polygamy is permitted and practised by them, and widowhood is not ordered to be preserved." In Bombay, in which considerable numbers of them have settled of late years, the Lowánás are principally traders and carriers of goods. Nothing peculiar is here observed as to the treatment of their women, except in the wise permission of second marriages. Their women, as will be seen from our photograph, share in the vigour of their race. Their costume is of a modest and graceful character, and numbers of them dispense with the noselet, which of native ornaments is least admired by Europeans. Their industry in Bombay is principally confined to their families, in which they enjoy more liberty than many of the females of other classes of the Hindus.

We have illustrated the costumes of the women, both of the upper and lower classes (the latter being represented by the figure on the left), as being the most characteristic. The men of the better class are scarcely distinguishable in their style of dress from the Bhátiás, except that the turbans of the former are a trifle smaller. A few of them have also adopted the broad flat head-dress worn by the Bráhmans of the Dakhan. The dress of the two women on the right is not unlike that of the Bhátiá female.

J. W.

No. 14.
LOWANA WOMEN.

SADHOOS.

(No. 15.)

NUMEROUS monastic orders exist in Goozerat, as in the other provinces of India. The Gosâees follow Shiva; they wear orange-tawny clothes, and the *teeluk*, or sectarian mark upon their foreheads, is horizontal. The Wairâgee is a Vaishnavite monk, and wears a white dress and a perpendicular *teeluk*. Those who are servants of the Devees, or local goddesses, add to the teeluk a *chándlo*, or red spot, made with a preparation of turmeric. The Jain monk is commonly called a Jutee, but the general name applying to all these orders is that of Sunyâsee, or anchorite. The Sunyâsees are now, for the most part, persons who have lost their property, have been deprived of their children, or suffered some other calamity, against which they have not had resolution to bear up. The intended recluse having arranged with a *Gooroo*, or monkish dignitary, for his reception into the order, and having ascertained the favourable day by astrological calculation, breaks the sacred cord, if he be of the regenerate classes, removes the hair of his head, assumes the monastic dress, and with alms and prayers receives initiation. Sunyâsees are, however, sometimes consecrated at an early age; a person who despairs of having children not unfrequently vows to consecrate one son, if two be granted to his prayers; and among the Jains, when disciples are scarce, as they frequently are, the monks purchase children for the purpose of initiating them.

The accompanying picture presents to view a group of ascetics called Sádhoos, one of whom gave the following account of himself:—

"I was born a Kunojeea Bráhman, at Mynpooree, on the Jumna. My father was Rámprusádjee, a Shám Vedist. About fifteen years ago I formed acquaintance with a Sádhoo, and from what I heard from him, I was seized with a desire for 'Chuktáee,' or religious wandering, and so I joined his fraternity, and have since performed pilgrimage to most of the Hindoo holy places. I am at present on my way to Beyt and Dwárká, and I intend afterwards to visit Wairág-Kshetra and the Bhál-Koond, near Prubhás, where Shree-Krishn was slain. Sádhoos employ themselves entirely in performing pilgrimages. They worship Shree-Krishn, and also other Hindoo deities. Marriage is customary among us; a Sádhoo's daughters are given to Sádhoos. If a Sádhoo take any other woman to wife than one of these, her hair is cut off, and she is admitted into the order. It is our custom to burn the dead, as is usual with other Hindoos. The Gooroo is the ruler of the order, and he has authority to exact whatever he pleases from his disciples. We dress as other Hindoos do, in the main, but we always wear *white* turbans and necklaces of toolshee. Occasionally Sádhoos wear a cap (topee), or wind a white cloth round their heads. Some Sádhoos play the Mouwur, or Morlee, musical instruments made of gourds, and employed in snake-charming. Some are Moonees, or speechless. They generally go about begging in parties of four or five, of whom the elder is treated as Mookhee, or Headman, but without perquisites."

A. K. F.

No 16.

SADHOOS.

KUMBHARS OF KUTCH.

(No. 16.)

KUMBHARS, or, in Sanskrit, Kumbhakáras, are the potters of India. In caste they rank somewhat below the Shúdras, or cultivators; but they have, nevertheless, a respectable position in the industrial community of India. In most villages (in the West of India, at any rate) they have an official connexion with the municipality, being obligated, on account of certain privileges and perquisites which they enjoy, to furnish earthen vessels on easy terms to the inhabitants, and to wait upon strangers, to supply them with water and appurtenances for holding it. They are generally very expert at their work, their appliances for which—a loaded moulding wheel (running horizontally on a pivot, which they turn rapidly by a stick), a knife, a string, with a quantity of kneaded clay—are extremely simple. Many of the vessels which they make are very neat, and partially ornamented. The Kutch potters are noted for the excellence of their work, sometimes applying smalt to such of the vessels which leave their hands as they do not wish to be porous. Sometimes they discharge the duties of the brickmaker, to which a separate caste (still existing in some parts of India) was assigned by the Hindus in ancient times. Our photograph gives specimens of their men, women, and children, in their better apparel, part of which they dispense with when at the wheel or kiln. The potters are not so friendly to the early formation of domestic establishments as some other castes; and they have more strength and vigour about them than many other parties originally of the same race. The females share in the work of their husbands, particularly in the matter of preparing the clay. It is only of late years that the Kutch potters began to settle in Bombay and its neighbourhood, where they are now much patronised. They have a small settlement at Bandora, in the island of Salsette.

J. W.

No. 16.

KHUMBARS OF KUTCH.

KHÁRÁVÁS.

(No. 17.)

THE Khárávás are a clan of Kolis from Gujarát, deriving their name from Kháro, salt, in the making of which they engage themselves in their native country. Many of them are boatmen and fishermen. Within the present century numbers of them have settled in Bombay, where they are engaged principally as cultivators (by the hoe, pickaxe, and billhook), and as layers and turners of tiles used in the roofing of houses. Our group represents five of them in their working costume, with some of their usual implements of labour. The Kolis, or Kulis (literally clansmen, from Kul, a clan), to which class of natives they belong, are closely allied to the Kulanbis, or Shúdra race; but many of them are but yet partially connected with Bráhmanism. The Khárávás, however, generally profess to be observers of Hinduism. They drink ardent spirits and freely use flesh and fish for food, but abstain from the slaughter of the cow, so sacred in the estimation of the modern Indians.

Nº 17.

KHÁRÁVÁS.

THE DHEDS OF GUJARÁT.

(No. 18.)

THE population of India Proper (overlooking the later immigrations) may be classed at least under three distinguishable races—that of the Japhetan A´rya, or ruling race, embracing the descendants of the Bráhmans, Kshatriyas, and Vaishyas, and the mixed classes which originated with it; the Shúdra, or servile race, probably cognate with the A´rya, and readily submitting to subordinate assimilation to it, but located in India before it; and the degraded Hamitic race, represented by the Dhéds or Dhers, of Gujarát, the Máhars or Parwárís, and Mángs, of the Maratha country, the Pariahs of the Madras Presidency, and their congeners in other provinces, whose ancestors were probably the first immigrants into India.

The appellation of Dhéd, applied to the tribe in Gujarát now alluded to, is probably a nickname, the precise meaning of which it is difficult to discover. It is, perhaps, a corruption of the word Darda, which, though originally the name of a non-Aryan people situated to the north of the affluents of the Indus, seems to have been applied to other peoples beyond the pale of Bráhmanism, elsewhere to be met with. The Western Vinásha (or Banás) river is represented in the Mahábhárata as hiding its face in the sands on approaching the impure country of the Abhirs, a people near the mouth of the Indus, and of the Dardas, who may be supposed to be also a non-Aryan people, in the neighbouring province of Gujarát—the Dhedas.

The Dhéds generally live in the exterior portions of the villages to which they belong, and are the drudges of all the other classes of the native community. Their touch, and even their shadow, are held to convey ceremonial defilement to the pure Hindu. To their own Turanian superstitions they have added many others, derived from the people among whom they dwell. The following notice of them is from the pen of a highly-esteemed and observant native missionary, the Rev. Dhanjibhai Nauroji:—

"They are clever to a certain extent, and, on the whole, industrious. The state of morality is very low among them. Cunning, deceit, and hypocrisy, are the chief elements in their character. Intemperance, and all its concomitant evils, have a great hold on them. Some of their customs are shocking to our feelings. They are superstitious to an incredible degree. In cases of illness and disease they trust more to the *mantras* and magical influence of their Gurus, or religious teachers, than to medicine. They worship all the idols of the Hindus, and many more that the latter do not know. Their Shástras, or scriptures, which recount to them the wondrous deeds of their Sádhus, or saints, are full of impure stories. Their Gurus are among the most ignorant, indolent, and vicious of beings. They rob and ruin these poor people. They make visits of several days to different families, whom they oblige not only to feed them, but to supply them with opium and other intoxicating drugs, to which they are greatly addicted. They are generally seen in the verandahs of different houses, with two baskets attached to each end of a pole, and covered with brown cloth. These baskets contain one or two small brass idols, a few shells, which are greatly adored, a piece of red cloth on which to spread these objects of worship, a bell to awaken their gods with, a piece of sandal-wood, and a small looking-glass, to help them in making marks on their foreheads, which they take care to make of enormous size, in order to show their greater sanctity. And how do these Gurus pass their time? In sleeping after a heavy repast, in smoking ganja, a narcotic drug, in repeating before men and women most impure tales, in singing wicked songs, in gambling with money they get from their followers, and the like. These are the men for whom the ignorant Dhéds cherish profound veneration, and whose mandates they dare not slight nor neglect!"

Great numbers of the Dhéds enter into the employment of Europeans in Bombay and Gujarát, especially as table servants, Masáls (taking charge of the lights and dishes of the family), and as horsekeepers and coachmen. Their comparative freedom from caste restrictions imposed upon themselves, and their readiness for different kinds of work, make them very serviceable to their masters.

Hopes of their elevation and improvement are founded on this fact. When employed by Europeans, they generally style themselves Suratis, or people of Surat. Our photograph of specimens of them, both men and women, illustrates their typical physiognomy, as well as shows their costume when they are in tolerably comfortable circumstances. They are generally copper-coloured, and not so black as many of the other aborigines of India. They are often well-developed in their bodily forms, and their countenances are marked by intelligence, if not by sagacity.

J. W.

Oriental Races and Tribes.

No 18.

THE DHEDS OF GUJARÁT.

WÂGHUREES.

(No. 19.)

WAGHUREES are a low caste of Hindoos, most of them originally from Marwar; but who are now found wandering about in every part of Goozerat under various mendicant disguises, the most common of which is that of the Sádhoo. Their legitimate occupation is hunting or snaring game; when disguised, however, they follow the occupation of the mendicants whom they represent. In the rains they betake themselves to Ahmedabad, or some one of the other large cities in Goozerat, which contain within their walls open spaces of ground fit for monsoon cultivation. In these positions the Wâghurees throw up little huts, which they soon surround with a garden of pumpkins, gourds, and the other vegetables which spring up rapidly during the rains, and which they sell in the market. The Ahmedabad Wâghurees are in the habit of hiring carts, with which they convey into the city for sale bricks dug up by them from among the ruins of old buildings, which extend for miles around the present city. It is commonly believed that while engaged in this occupation they frequently find and appropriate valuable hidden treasure, and that they are, in consequence, very wealthy. The ordinary dress of the Wâghurees, in their hunting capacity, is given in the accompanying picture. They are followers of a Bhugut, who founded a religious sect called that of the Beej Punt. The object of their worship is the monkey-god Hunoomân. They do not intermarry with other castes, and are careful to have their marriages celebrated by a Bráhman; but they permit of the second marriage of women. They bury the dead. Numbers of them have been long settled in Bombay as beggars and street musicians; but it is from among the few who annually visit the island to dispose of the peacocks and wild fowls they have snared alive that our illustration has been drawn.

A. K. F.

No 19.

WÂGHUREES.

PÁRSÍS.

(Nos. 20 and 21.)

THE word Parsee, or rather Pársí, as it is written by our Orientalists, is the Eastern word for a Persian. It is not applied in India, however, to the present natives of Persia—who are most commonly denominated Irání (Iranians), or Moghals, from their dominant tribe—but to the descendants of a portion of Zoroastrians, who have now for many centuries been settled on our own shores. "The ancestors of the Pársís of Western India," says Dr. Wilson, in one of his works on their religion, "were a portion of the followers of Zoroaster, who fled from their homes in Persia on its invasion by the Musalman Khalifs in the middle of the seventh century of the Christian era. It appears (from their own accounts) that they retreated, in the first instance, to the mountains of Khorásán, where they continued for a hundred years; that they afterwards proceeded to Hormazd, or Ormus, in the Persian Gulf, where they remained for fifteen years, during which they prepared several vessels intended for facilitating their further emigration; that after finally leaving the shores of their native country, they first landed in Diva, or Dieu, a small island to the south-west of the Peninsula of Gujarát, where they were contented to remain for nineteen years, during which they acquired a knowledge of the Hindu languages and handicrafts; and that on the expiry of that time they set sail for Sanján, at the southern extremity of the Gujarát province." They were not long in India before they connected themselves with its arts, agriculture, and commerce. The attachment of the Pársís to commercial business, indeed, is so strong, that Professor Westergaard thinks that it was one of the principal motives which originally brought them to these shores. The commerce of Surat made that city for a considerable time their head-quarters, which have now, however, been removed to Bombay, where they occupy a very prominent place in the native community, as merchants, bankers, shipbuilders, brokers, shopkeepers, contractors, and mechanics. The first native of India on whom Her Majesty conferred the honour of knighthood and a baronetcy, as all the world knows, was a Pársí—the late munificent Jamsetjee Jejeebhoy. The Pársís, too, have been among the first to enter the learned professions in India. They have proved not the least successful students of medicine at the Grant Medical College; and the first commission in the regular Medical Service of the East India Company was gained, through honourable competition, by one of their number. Two of them, converted to Christianity, were, a few years ago, ordained to the Christian ministry in connexion with the Free Church of Scotland. Several of them are at present vigorously prosecuting the study of law. A few of them have established themselves as mercantile agents in London, where one of them is a professor of the Gujarátí language in University College. It augurs well for them, as a body, that they are beginning to estimate aright the benefits of female education and elevation. Their priests have scarcely kept pace in advancement with the lay-members of their community. These priests, properly speaking, are divided into two orders, Mobeds and Herbads, though Dasturs (corresponding with our doctors in divinity) are also recognised by them. The matter which divides the Pársís has reference merely to the observance, or non-observance, of an intercalary month, leading to the choice of different days for their religious festivals. The word Mobed, we should add, in further explanation, is derived from the Zend word Máoghípaiti, a Master-Magus; and Herbad from the Zend word Airyapaiti, a master of the Airyas. The word Airya is the name, or denomination, of the ancient seat of the Zoroastrians. For information on the faith and practices of the Zoroastrians, see "The Pársí Religion," by the Rev. Dr. Wilson; and "Essays on the Sacred Language, Writings, and Religion of the Pársís," by Dr. Martin Haug.

Oriental Races and Tribes.

No. 20.
PARSÍS.

Oriental Races and Tribes.

No 21

PÁRSÍ WOMEN.

MEHMANS.

(Nos. 22 and 23.)

THE Mehmans, or rather Mihmans—for the word is derived from the Persian Mihman, a stranger or guest—are converts to the Suni form of the Muhammadan religion, principally from the agricultural and mercantile classes of the Hindus of Kutch and Káthiáwár. Their position in the native community is very similar to that of the Khojas, who are Shias. In Kutch and Káthiáwár many of them are cultivators; but in Bombay, with the exception of a few who have acquired wealth and risen to the position of shipowners and merchants, they are mostly shopkeepers and pedlars. The parties in our photograph are principally vendors of books, the comparative value of which they know only from the existing demand.

The Mehmans make pilgrimages to Mecca and other shrines in Arabia sacred to Muhammadans, and the title of Haji (pilgrim) may be found prefixed to a great many Mehman names in Bombay. The females frequently accompany them on these pilgrimages.

There is nothing peculiar in the costume of the Mehmans, though, of course, the green turban—the symbol of professed descent from the Prophet—is not to be seen among them. They appear more vigorous than the Hindu races, with whom they are on a level. Education, properly so called, has made but comparatively little progress among them. In Bombay they speak the Gujarátí and Kutchí languages.

The Mehman women are often rather gaily dressed. They have adopted the *izár*, or trousers, of Musalman females. Their Indian origin is pretty distinctly marked by their soft countenances and clear eyes. They walk about the streets without the reserve and envelopement of Muhammadan women in general; but they seldom undertake outdoor work for hire. They maintain a good deal of intercourse with their Hindu neighbours, when they are permitted to do so by the etiquette of caste. School education has as yet made no progress among them, though it is making rapid advancement among various classes of Indian females.

J. W.

No. 22.

MEHMANS.

No 23.

MEHMAN WOMEN.

KHOJAHS.

(No. 24.)

THE Khojahs of the West of India are converts to the Shia form of the Muhammedan faith from the Hindu natives of Gujarát, Káthiáwár, and Kutch, made principally within the last three centuries. They take their name from one of the titular appellations of one of their earlier instructors: properly it means a eunuch, or party in authority. The present religious head of the majority of their community is Agha Khan Mahomed Husein Huseini, the son-in-law of the late Fatteh Ali, Shah of Persia. He is much reverenced by his followers; but the reform party, which is daily becoming more and more influential in Bombay, is not altogether satisfied with his administration.

The Khojah population of Bombay amounts to 6,000; of Gujarát, to 5,000; of Káthiáwár, to 20,000; of Kutch, to 3,000. Some of its members are settled in the Persian Gulf and at Zanzibar. The Khojahs are principally employed as merchants and petty dealers. Shoemaking is the only handicraft followed by any of them. They have lately showed a charitable spirit, and some of them, headed by Dharamsí Punjabhai, a wealthy merchant, and a man of most liberal mind, are doing much in support of education, though not without serious opposition from the olden school. They had for some time a Gujarátí newspaper of their own called the *Khojah Dost*, or *Khojah Friend*, but this has been lately amalgamated with the *Satya Dipika*, or *Lamp of Truth.*

His Highness the Agha has answered the complaints made against himself as an anti-reformer, by sending his son-in-law to the Free General Assembly's Institution, in Bombay, where he is regarded with interest by all his teachers. This well-known patriarch is a great patron of the turf, and deals largely in race-horses of the finest breeds, which he imports from Persia and Arabia.

The central figure in our group is Nansi Parpia ("Old Nancy," as he is called at times), of shopkeeping celebrity in Bombay, whose kind, accommodating disposition is known to many of our British youths in the commencement of their Indian career. His companion in the honours of the chair is the founder of one of the Khojah firms recently established in London. In the elder of the two youths represented in our picture we have an excellent type of "Young Bombay." Every article of his dress bears unmistakable evidence of the anxiety of his class to assimilate the Oriental to the English costume.

J. W.

Nº 24.

KHOJAHS.

MUHAMMADAN WOMEN OF SURAT.

(No. 25.)

THE position of Surat, about 180 miles north of Bombay, is well known. It is a very ancient city; for long it was the principal seaport on the West of India of the Great Moghal, and the principal commercial mart of the European nations. In consequence of this circumstance, it contains more than the usual proportion of Muhammadans. They are of various countries and provinces; but of late years they have begun to amalgamate by intermarriage. Their females, except in the few higher families of the place, are not so secluded as Musalman women are in many other parts of India; and few or no inconveniences are the result, notwithstanding the legal facilities of divorce and polygamy of the community to which they belong. Our photograph represents individuals of the middle classes of society, in their ordinary dress, which is of a much more modest character than that of many Indian females. The ornamented frontlet will be noticed as a peculiarity. Such parties as those who are here set forth are by no means destitute of intelligence, though they have not the advantage of a school education. It is to be regretted that while female education is making great progress among both Pársís and Hindus in the West of India, it is but little regarded by the Muhammadans. A movement in its favour is much to be desiderated.

J. W.

Nº 25

MUHAMMADAN WOMEN OF SURAT.

BOHORAS.

(No. 26.)

THE Bohoras, properly so called, are a sect of Muhammadans, corresponding in many respects with the Ismailiyah, the Ansairiyah, the Mutawilah, and the Drusis of Syria. They pay particular regard to the tenets of Ismail ibn Jáfar, the Sixth Imam, and hold, like the Shias, but in a more exaggerated form, the mystical doctrine of the union of the Deity with Ali. They are amongst the first converts to Muhammadanism in the West of India, but the exact time of their abandonment of Hinduism is unknown. Their earliest teachers are said to have come to India—to Khambát, or Cambay (in Gujarát)—in the first instance, in the eleventh century of the Christian era. Their present Mullahs, or pontiffs, are of Arabian descent, and claim to be of the offspring of Muhammad himself.

Most of the Bohoras are pedlars, shopkeepers, and workers in iron and tin. Numbers of them, however—particularly in the district of Broach—are agriculturists, whose ancestors, under the patronage of the Muhammadan princes of Gujarát, seceded from Shiahism, and became Sunis.

The mercantile Bohoras—the real original Bohoras—are divided into three sects, which derive their names—the Suleimání, the Aliyah, and the Dawudiyah—from certain lines of the Mullahs to whom they adhere.

The Suleimánís are not a numerous body. In Surat they had only fifty families a few years ago. In Baroda they had, at the same time, 250 houses, while at Haidarábád, in the Dakhan, they were still more numerous. The Chief Mullah of this sect resides in Arabia, but he has a representative in India, who travels about the country, having his head-quarters at Baroda.

The Aliyah are a still smaller sect than the Suleimánís.

The Dawudiyah is by far the largest sect of Bohoras. In Surat, in 1829, they had 2,500 houses. They are to be found in other towns of Gujarát and Kutch, and in Bombay, Puná, Ahmadnagar, Burhánpor, Aurangábád, Haidarábád, Indor, Ujjayin, &c., &c. Their Mullah is a person of much consequence, receiving honorary titles short of those of the Divinity. His deputies too, enjoy much respect, and even act for him at some of the Arabian ports. He encourages Arabic learning, but he has not yet shown any great countenance to the progress of general enlightenment among his flock. He appoints his successor after the professed revelation of the name of the proper party in a dream.

Notwithstanding the religious enthusiasm by which the Bohoras are characterised, and their devotion to their Mullahs, they are a very peaceable class of the Indian community, and in this respect very unlike their co-religionists in other Muhammadan countries.

The dress of the Bohoras is generally pretty uniform; as far, especially, as the male portion of their community is concerned. The men generally wear plain white turbans, and angrakhas, or coats, and striped trousers. In the photograph they are represented in their ordinary dress. On great occasions the angrakha is exchanged for the jámá (coat) and waistband, or zone, worn by the Darbár attendants of Muhammadan princes and nobles; and this dress, it may here be remarked, is the holiday costume alike of Pársís, Muhammadans, Parbhus, and other classes of the Hindu community. For the dress of the women we must refer to our illustration. Their aversion to the *izár*, or trousers, worn by Muhammadan women in general, is supposed to be connected with their Indian descent.

Various interesting notices of the Bohoras are to be found in Briggs' "Cities of Gujarashtra," and in the *Oriental Christian Spectator* for April, 1848.

J. W.

Oriental Races and Tribes.

No 26

BOHORAS.